ALSO BY JOHN SUROWIECKI

BOOKS

Burger King of the Dead
Martha Playing Wiffle Ball in Her Wedding Dress and Other Poems
Flies; or, the Last Days, D___h and Putrefaction of Mr. Sam Jeden as
        Narrated by 8 Generations of Musca Domestica
Barney and Gienka
The Hat City After Men Stopped Wearing Hats
Watching Cartoons Before Attending a Funeral

CHAPBOOKS

Missing Persons
Mr. Z., Mrs. Z., J.Z., S.Z.
Bolivia Street
Further Adventures of My Nose
Dennis Is Transformed into a Thrush
Five-hundred Widowers in a Field of Chamomile
Caliban Poems

The Place
of the Solitaires

The Place
of the Solitaires

Poems from Titles by Wallace Stevens

John Surowiecki

Julie —
It was a pleasure
reading with you.
Let's do it again
some time.
Good luck in your
writing!

JSurow
4·20·22

Wolfson Press
2022

Volume editor, John Cassels
Cover and interior design by Sky Santiago
Copyright © 2022 by John Surowiecki
All rights reserved. First edition.

ISBN: 978-1950066117

Wolfson Press
Master of Liberal Studies Program
Indiana University South Bend
1700 Mishawaka Avenue
South Bend, Indiana 46634-7111
WolfsonPress.com

Contents

Acknowledgments

Author's Note

Invective against Swans..3
The Plot against the Giant..4
Nuances of a Theme by Williams...5
From the Misery of Don Joost..6
Anecdote of the Prince of Peacocks..7
The Place of the Solitaires..8
Colloquy with a Polish Aunt...9
The Man Whose Pharynx Was Bad...10
The Revolutionists Stop for Orangeade...11
The Public Square..12
The Sun This March..13
A Fish-Scale Sunrise...14
Loneliness in Jersey City..15
The Blue Buildings in the Summer Air...16
Mrs. Alfred Uruguay..18
Men Made Out of Words...19
Large Red Man Reading...20
The Woman in Sunshine...21
Puella Parvula..22
An Ordinary Evening in New Haven..23
An Old Man Asleep...24
Vacancy in the Park..25
Final Soliloquy of the Interior Paramour.......................................26
The River of Rivers in Connecticut..27
A Child Asleep in Its Own Life..28

Notes..31

Acknowledgments

The author is grateful to the editors of the following publications in which some of the poems first appeared, some in slightly different forms.

The Chronicle (Willimantic, Connecticut): "Anecdote of the Prince of Peacocks"; "A Fish-Scale Sunrise."
Garden: "The Sun This March."
The Louisville Review: "An Old Man Asleep."
SLAB: "An Ordinary Evening in New Haven."
Typishly Literary Magazine: "The Place of the Solitaires."
The Southern Review: "The Blue Buildings in the Summer Air."
The Wallace Stevens Journal: "Large Red Man Reading"; "Men Made Out of Words"; "The River of Rivers in Connecticut."

Special thanks to Daniel Donaghy, Debbie Gilbert, Nick Mougey, and the members of the East-West Writing Group (Storrs, Connecticut).

For Denise, Vanessa, John, and Mike: with Love

AUTHOR'S NOTE:

The following poems are not imitations of Stevens's poems but departures from them, using his usually inventive titles as launching pads. My intent is not to address the matter of the poems (although sometimes that can't be helped) but to create personal, mostly sublunary counterparts, each producing a solid thump as it goes from his rarefied geography to my more ordinary one.

Invective against Swans

Public Gardens, Boston

Where we once raised our voices against a war,
    where children—the dukes of ducks and queens
    of butterflies—once slept on blankets stuck
like stamps on an envelope of lawn,
we welcome back all the old Lohengrins

who go down to the sea in Swan Boats,
    catamarans in diarrheal water, itching for a fight.
    There's still time, boys: take the Green Line.
Plenty of souls to save and wrongs to right
and grails on sale at Crate & Barrel.

THE PLOT AGAINST THE GIANT

The seed of hatred, planted in everyone,
blossoms in some, sometimes in most.

The monster lives where death is simplest,
where there's room enough at last for sleep.

Those who live nearby can hear
the final whimpers of creatures

crushed by the weight of sky
as it suddenly descends and forces

the life from them. Most believe
even a giant's sweetest voice is seismic,

while there are those who contend
a giant presents no danger at all.

All it wants is a consistency of size,
a justice of scale. All it wants

is a guarantee of nothing underfoot
and words large enough to read,

a language that names everything it sees
and disregards what it's forced to imagine.

NUANCES OF A THEME BY WILLIAMS

It is not fair to be old,
to put on a brown sweater.
When the good doctor says brown
he means the color of gravy as in

gravy train: and in the sweater's weave
he can feel the comfort of bringing in
wood on the first cold day
in November or watching trees

waltz recklessly in the wind,
knowing that if they fall
they'll find sleep
in their own dead leaves.

Old age brings no surprises:
poetry lives elsewhere—and nowhere
is there a regard for gain or loss.
Its calculator only subtracts

and the past is nothing outside the memory of it,
tableaux of victories
no one cares about, secrets
no one will ever know.

And what is death but the last afternoon nap?
What needs to be done has been done,
what needs to be forgotten
already goes unrecalled.

From the Misery of Don Joost

In the end no one's afraid of him,
the pipsqueak, algorithm of bones, sum of
uric throbs and stabbings behind
        the eyeballs.

No one wants to listen to his bullshit.
Giants turn out to be grain silos
and cell towers,
monsters are pets that get somehow
        rearranged.

And life? Life is
whatever anyone says it is,
then turns to pain no matter
        what they say.

ANECDOTE OF THE PRINCE OF PEACOCKS

for John

A man walks into a bar and orders a shot,
so someone shoots him.

The slug goes through his heart
and gets lodged in the jukebox,

causing all the songs to play at once.
The room is suddenly filled with dancers.

Every refrain of every song contains
the cries of a lost child, which tend to dampen

the party atmosphere. Later, peahens
peck out the eyes of the inattentive

and deposit them in spittoons
conveniently located at either end of the bar.

That won't stop the dancing though.
One man has already maxed out his Visa,

strutting and pretending he has feathers to display.
The women only smile and shake their heads.

The Place of the Solitaires

We're desperate for the touch
of a glove or a sleeve or a lapel.
That's all we ask: proximity to
anything that's not us or ours.
We live where families are sad
jittery movies of themselves.
Friends are rampaging rivers
bringing us end tables and night tables
and breakfast bars with one stool.
It seems every closet in the world
vomits up clothes we can wear.
As for the young woman who lives
nearby and paints her nails in
different colors in no discernible
pattern: knowing her name would
be the same as marrying her.
Once she waved at us in the space
between our houses and I dreamed
of her hand for nearly a year.
There are no rivals where we live.
We chip away at the lichen of
our loneliness, our skin and home.
We have little else to offer each other.
We know we have no chance of winning:
no one will ever take us or want to.

COLLOQUY WITH A POLISH AUNT

I

Jailor of our childhoods,
she sets free the days
we've forgotten or never knew,
days that never really mattered.

II

She says it's vodka that makes her nose big
and whiskey that keeps it red.
She's already outlived some of us:
the rest she doesn't care about.

III

She says whenever we speak of her
we circle our ears with our fingers.
She's our *coitka*, but she says
we barely touch when we embrace.

IV

All you want are charming stories
of innocence and mischievousness.
Otherwise, the past has nothing to say to you.
Sorrow is loss and you've lost nothing.

The Man Whose Pharynx Was Bad

The voice in the brown box
belongs to someone at the VA
hospital, the resonant baritone
one might expect from a soldier,
a man of few words answering
FAQs on what to do to win,
how big the payoff is, when the
drawing will take place. Silence
is now absolute. Its memorial
is this card table at this corner
of the Stop & Shop parking lot,
this lasso of red raffle tickets,
this cupful of cheap pens,
this brown box and the voice
inside it which most people
think is his. What no one wants
to know is how his voice was
lost or why or what he sounded
like when he was a young man
or what thoughts have escaped him
and flown away—fly away still—
never rooted in speech.

The Revolutionists Stop for Orangeade

Someone builds ziggurats
of Valencias as what?
a hobo-sign of sympathy?

a notice to all that what's
drunk here is not
from concentrate?

This is just a stopover,
brother, a breather.
The march goes well, thanks,

the fire still burns inside us.
In you that fervor takes a more
liquid and nourishing form:

but all to the same end, right?
No amount of freedom can
satisfy the parched masses.

Oh, we agree, we agree—
the loudest of us should be
trusted least of all.

Too much irrefutable logic,
not enough frailty and indecision,
which is what we understand

best and why we stop
in the first place.
We thirst, bro, we thirst.

The Public Square

The horses go one way, the generals another,
and while parts survive—a gloved hand, a swatch of mane,
balls painted blue and gold by college boys—wholes vanish.

In time other statues appear: a nurse, a teller,
a bartender making Manhattans, the kid at the A&P,
an X-ray tech, a rowing team, someone's visiting cousin,

someone talked about but rarely seen, a bus driver,
a tax advisor, a dental hygienist reborn in her own light,
a pediatrician, life-size horseflies, a cod in a cube of sea.

The Sun This March

We are vaccinated, soldiers baring arms,
and the sunlight is—not warmer,
never that—but less hostile, asking, not insisting,

that winter leave us at last,
returning days with faces
and voices that warm

in the resonance of other voices,
unraveling jokes, recounting
brilliant escapades and foolish theories.

Because it was winter last summer and winter last spring
and winter when the irises bloomed
the color of wounds and iodine.

And the drought that killed them
was nothing less than a blizzard, static and brown,
and the fall that announced winter was winter,

and the winter that came was more winter than winter,
with frozen air and house-
high snow and daggered trees.

And now we squint and tear
and find shadows everywhere,
watching where we walk

for just-born hornets or waxy hyacinths.
Now we find our gloves preposterous
and our boots leaden

and with a flourish unwind our school-
striped scarves and cram them
into our pockets.

A Fish-Scale Sunrise

for Barney

My father liked to say he
once served Judy Garland:
vodka and grapefruit juice
and, later on, Coke. It seems
she liked Coke. He said she
was twitchy, smoked what

he smoked, talked a lot but,
to his surprise, about him,
not herself, about his wife,
his day job at the Aircraft,
about me, off to college to study
chemistry—the mixology of

the universe, which made her
crack a smile. She promised to be
his *paloma blanca* celebrating
the birth of another day. She
ordered haddock, New England-
style, Ritz-cracker-crusted,

milky flesh auguring a tornado
in Kansas, a room in London,
and a night soon to end with clouds
interlocking in rows of scales
that only a first shift's first light
can scrape away.

LONELINESS IN JERSEY CITY

Here we are in Chilltown
looking at the glass Chopin
with a manatee of a man
in a three-piece suit

who says sure why not
to a shot or two or three
of Four Roses: pretty soon
he's totally fucked up

and no longer cares if
we think it's *all* all right.
Not much you can expect
from a Harvard man

and a Hartford man.
Life's only an idea to him,
an enigma, maybe a chimera,
a comfort nonetheless.

We're not the ones
made out of words:
we make the tables
he puts his planets on.

THE BLUE BUILDINGS IN THE SUMMER AIR

I

Crystalline buildings appeared one day
and new blue light poured through them.
The old neighborhoods vaporized in the glare.
That summer, the Roma settled in Hartford
handing out futures by the train station,
and soon everyone was rich
and famous and desperately in love.

II

A new plaza returned the new light in blue waves.
A new cathedral grew out of a moss of familiar houses,
closer than anything else to the end of things.

In June we passed each other on the street,
a goofy kid and an obese poet in a gray suit.
The future was tidy and sequenced and sapphirine,
even for the poet whose end was a month or two away.

III

He imagined the offices inside the blue buildings,
cleared the desks of photos and knickknackery,

ordered lively posters in cold chrome frames—
a show of Mondrian's watercolors,
a look at Picasso during the war—

and there he was, drinking rare teas and talking into
a streamlined Dictaphone with blinking blue lights.

IV

And the blue buildings had blue shadows which
children chased around the plaza.

There were blue lights at Christmas, too, self-
illuminating snow with Mozart in the air free of charge.

And the blue buildings were content to be moderately tall
and July-blue in July, the flimsiest of blues, recalling the skies
in places where crops were paid attention to.

V

Maybe he smiled at me as I walked by,
smiled and nodded as if to say he was
just an ordinary man living an ordinary life
in an extraordinary world where everyone

was an artist no matter what, and here was where
that life began, in these buildings with blue skins
that blue light was passing through.

MRS. ALFRED URUGUAY

She became a citizen of him,
a man of affluent beaches
and gated orchards.
She was his pledge of allegiance

and unfurling flag:
blue and white stripes
with a sun in the corner,
with his face and no other's in the sun.

He was the nation of first husbands
watching the world go by north of him,
waving from a ship
that never sailed.

It was love at third
or fourth or fifth sight:
he was the land of fire
between oceans, themselves

aflame and unquenchable.
How exciting to find her name on a map
as if her love for him
were a sort of treasure.

MEN MADE OUT OF WORDS

Everyone please stop writing for a few days.
  Let the brilliance settle like dust on the tops
of pianos and bookshelves.

Let words become a cuneiform
  of dead worms on ordinary sidewalks,
sentences become odors no one recognizes.

Words give way, aren't the way, get in the way.
  Each one is a double entendre,
so what is is now twice what it used to be.

Whatever you think your life is, it's not that:
  not anything of a shape or color anymore,
not anything you can put into so many words.

Large Red Man Reading

The sagacious man who smells of beets
and rust has always been beset by ghosts,
           but not large red ones.

Someone's lost sister brushes October leaves
from his red shoulders; someone's uncle,
           for whom the crossword

is a university, helps him with the want ads.
He learns about Prospero, who hides from the Red
           Death but dies anyway,

and he thinks about the world none of us is meant to see
and the type of time that's not made for passing
           and doesn't age a soul one bit.

THE WOMAN IN SUNSHINE

for Denise

Even on the coldest day, as you sit reading
in the embrace of your chair, the light pulls
fragrances from your skin, draws out
radiances of heliotrope, still dormant,
waiting in theory at least to live again.
Getting up, you unfold like a peony:
winter light is summer heat almost
and you collect it to make spring.

PUELLA PARVULA

for Vanessa

When you were three you nonchalantly walked into
the deep end of a swimming pool. Luckily,
I fished you out before you touched bottom,
before you even realized you were afraid.

    This happened in the season
    of memory, so we shivered
    all the way home.

I also remember your blue velvet dress
and your sandbox under the moon
and the Armenian storekeeper who gave you treats
because the sun never left your hair.

    One day sidewalk milkweeds
    coughed up monarchs and concords peek-
    a-booed behind a neighbor's garage.

And one day we rode the bus into the city
standing with patients from the asylum, and when
you, unable to hold it in any longer, peed on the floor,

    one man smiled and said tragedies happen
    even on the Belmont bus and dammed
    the flow with his scarred black shoes.

An Ordinary Evening in New Haven

I

Once a waitress named Bobbi (she liked
Roberta) invited me to her flat off Dixwell Ave.
It had no kitchen to speak of.

II

Her windows rattled despite being taped.
Her wallpaper, zinnias helixing,
made winter bearable for her.

III

She smelled like cigarillos. She was burned in a fire
and the skin along her back felt like the ribbed
withdrawing skin of a worm.

IV

She said love was a statue made of air, a garden
without soil. Only the anticipation that preceded it,
the longing for it, the need for it, were real.

V

And so were the bitterness and penance that
followed it and now and then the sense that
you'd been robbed of everything you ever owned.

VI

On her walls were postcard prints of Chagalls.
She wrote poems about her sick mother.
She wrote a poem for me and later tore it up.

An Old Man Asleep

Volcanoes spit out clouds of teachers.
The sea gives up children, his and maybe his,
getting sick on sundaes and root beer.
Beach roads are crowded with old friends.

One by one they tell him he won't die.
No disease will take him, no accident will befall him.
Nothing will end with him,
just one beginning after another

and all that time to think about all that time
and all those times needing to be made right,
life to reassess and loves to leave
exactly as they were.

VACANCY IN THE PARK

When we sense a hole in the air
or an icy shadow or the arrhythmic
skip of a universal heart,
it's because she's left the park,

no one knows where to exactly, maybe off
to encourage lovers rendezvousing at happy hour
or already naked behind the forsythia.

When she's gone, children with hat-
flattened hair read online confessions of serial killers
and, looking up, cheer on dogs as they

race through backyard spiderworts,
sniffing out epochs of their history.
Folks report on her whereabouts and are usually wrong.
          But when she's here, it's June.

The roses explode and implode
and explode again: bloom and a-bloom
and a-bloom-bloom-bloom.
O it's always so good to see her!

We have lunch at the café
—she loves her *linguine con vongole*—
then she'll drop in on a wedding or two,

posing with bridesmaids and best men.
She always drinks too much and I have to
hold her by her collar by a greenhouse door.

When she pukes it's pink from cosmos
—not the drinks from the open bar and not
the gangling daisy-like annuals, but one of the ways
          to say everything there is.

FINAL SOLILOQUY OF THE INTERIOR PARAMOUR

Is this the *this is it?* the unfriendly end of it all,
the last step of our plodding parade? Let's begin
                    at the beginning.

Where's my choo-choo? Will anyone
ever decode my secret message?
                    8-9, 13-15-13!

What delights most is what's fading fastest,
no longer within reach, a nuance followed by a hint,
                    a trace of a trace.

Now I live for a birdcall, an m&m, the sight of you.
Now I'm told to breathe just to remember what
                    it's like to breathe.

Whole years drown in tears, every third thought
is on should-have-beens and ought-to-bes.
                    Time doesn't go

on holiday: time is time-and-a-half *in aeternum*,
forever on the clock. Bones rattle in my throat,
                    but I don't mourn

anyone. I mourn lost time. I mourn wretchedness
and weeping and heartache. I mourn the vacuum,
                    not the voyage.

THE RIVER OF RIVERS IN CONNECTICUT

In memoriam: Joe Cary

We always found our way back to the gaiety of it,
satires of exigencies, flashes in the sun.
But his river was never quite ours, was it?
    Or anyone else's.

See Farmington from the riverbank? Not a chance.
No ferryman? Actually, there are two,
one in Glastonbury, one in Chester (plus
    there's the knot in Windsor to consider).

Down in Haddam men don't
imagine golden birds, but they often
get to see eagles. Current tends to
    spill thickly there, sediment and dross.

In spring, freshets are
easily managed, compliant,
familiar. Taken together,
    it's one big blue-brown cocktail.

In winter it begins as
one thing and ends as another,
carrying sticks and snow
    to the sound of sounds

and the Race of Races, the sea of seas and the key of keys,
where the poet of poets ignores icy innuendos
and digs his feet deeper
    into venereal sand.

A Child Asleep in Its Own Life

The angel is only me, eating an Almond Joy
behind the ottoman.
If I say I've come down from heaven,
you'll only laugh and tell me
to stop being such a jerk.

I'm also the golden crow that you think lives in
a cage of your making and the kindly red worm
that's been slithering for so long
its belly has gone tender and leaks
the paths it travels on.

I'm no water baby, though: too old.
You'll be one soon because
it's the in-between age,
the years of underwater mischief
and slippery bravado.

As a water baby you can hide in reeds
and figure out who's who and what's what.
But until then, you're vapor,
your own breath, a breeze that tickles leaves
and wrinkles lakes.

You enter and exit your own lungs,
redden and ride your own blood.
You are the sigh between kisses
and the small semi-snotty laugh
escaping through your nose.

NOTES

"Colloquy with a Polish Aunt"
coitka
Polish for aunt.

"A Fish-Scale Sunrise"
the Aircraft
Pratt & Whitney Aircraft, a division of United Technologies, a
major employer in Connecticut.

paloma blanca
The white dove in the song, "La Paloma," mentioned in the Stevens
poem.

a tornado / in Kansas, a room in London
It's said that a tornado roared through Kansas on the day Judy
Garland died—in a room in London.

"Loneliness in Jersey City"
the glass Chopin
The glass ceiling portrait of Frederic Chopin in the White Eagle
Hall in Jersey City (a.k.a. Chilltown). In the Stevens poem: "There's
nothing whatever to see / Except Polacks that pass in their motors /
And play concertinas all night."

"The Blue Buildings in the Summer Air"
That summer, the Roma settled in Hartford
In the 1950s, the Roma were frequent visitors to Hartford, although
they weren't welcomed by city officials. At one point, the City
Council made it difficult for them to make a living by banning
"character readings"—a euphemism for fortune-telling.

"Vacancy in the Park"
The park in this poem—and probably Stevens's—is Elizabeth Park
in Hartford. The poet's favorite refuge, it was named for Elizabeth
Pond, a banker's wife and decidedly not the carousing spirit in this
version.

"The River of Rivers in Connecticut"
   the Race of Races
   The Race is an area of the Atlantic with deep waters and strong
   currents and serves as a nautical gateway to the Long Island Sound.

The text of this book is set in Adobe Caslon by Carol Twombly (1990). It is a digital revival of the font originally designed by William Caslon (1722).

The front cover font, ITC Founders Caslon (also used for the main title on the full-title page), is a distressed digital revival of Caslon's original letterpress font. It was designed by Justin Howes (1998). Here, it serves to replicate the text of Wallace Stevens's first book, *Harmonium* (Knopf 1923).

Made in the USA
Monee, IL
30 March 2022

93249653R10031